Women of the Civil War

by Eric Michaels

Table of Contents

Getting Started 2
Sojourner Truth 4
Julia Ward Howe 7
Harriet Tubman 10
Clara Barton 13
Index 16

capstone classroom

Getting Started

Today in the United States, we all enjoy freedom. That wasn't always the case. In the 1800s women had very few rights. Many people were held as slaves. At that time life in the United States was very different than it is today.

In 1861 the United States began fighting the Civil War (1861–1865). The northern states and southern states fought against each other. Life in the South was very different from life in the North. The southern states wanted slavery to continue, but the northern states did not. This was one of the reasons the states began fighting against each other.

Abraham Lincoln was president during the Civil War.

This was a very difficult time in the United States. Many brave people stood up for what they believed was right.

Let's see how four brave women made a difference during the Civil War years.

Sojourner Truth

Sojourner Truth was born into a family of slaves in New York around 1797. She was named Isabella.

In 1826 she ran away to escape slavery. The next year, slavery ended in the state of New York. Isabella was finally free!

In the early 1840s, Isabella became a speaker. She also changed her name to Sojourner Truth. She was the first black woman to speak out against slavery.

Sojourner made speeches about women's rights. She also talked about ending slavery everywhere.

In 1864 Sojourner Truth met President Abraham Lincoln.

During the Civil War, many slaves went north looking for freedom. Sojourner did what she could to help them. She even met with President Lincoln and shared her feelings about slavery with him.

Sojourner Truth

Sojourner Truth died in 1883. She used the power of words to fight for what she believed was right.

Julia Ward Howe

Julia Ward was born in New York City in 1819. In 1843 she married a doctor, Samuel Gridley Howe. He spent much of his time helping others. Julia helped her husband work to end slavery.

During the Civil War, the Howes visited soldiers in Virginia. Julia heard the soldiers singing a song. It caught her attention. She couldn't get the tune out of her head. She decided to write new words for that tune.

Julia Ward Howe

The song Julia wrote, "Battle Hymn of the Republic," became famous. Her song was printed in a magazine. The song became popular with Union soldiers in the Northern army. Many other people liked it too.

After the Civil War ended, Julia worked for women's rights and other causes she cared about. Even today her "Battle Hymn of the Republic" is sung as a patriotic song.

Harriet Tubman

Harriet Tubman was born into a family of slaves around 1820. She worked in the fields and as a house servant.

Harriet used the Underground Railroad to escape to freedom in 1849. This wasn't a real railroad. It was a system of different places, such as houses and barns, where slaves could hide. They stopped at the secret places as they escaped to the North.

Harriet wanted to help others escape along the Underground Railroad. She helped about 300 slaves escape to freedom, including her own family.

Harriet Tubman

    During the Civil War, Harriet worked for the Union army as a nurse. She also worked as a scout, or spy. Even as the fighting went on, Harriet bravely helped slaves escape to freedom.

Harriet Tubman (far left) with some of the people she helped.

After the Civil War ended, Harriet raised money for schools. She also began a home for people in need. Today the Harriet Tubman Home still stands in New York.

Clara Barton

Clara Barton was born in 1821 in Massachusetts. As a young woman she worked as a teacher.

When the Civil War began, Clara wanted to help. She took supplies to soldiers on the battlefields. She helped men who were hurt. Clara soon became known as the "Angel of the Battlefield."

After the war Clara went to Switzerland. While she was there, she learned about the Red Cross. The Red Cross was a group that helped people in times of war.

Clara Barton

   Clara wanted the United States to have a Red Cross too. In 1881 she opened an American Red Cross office. People could get help from the American Red Cross at any time, not just during a war.

Clara Barton's house

Clara Barton died in 1912. But the Red Cross lives on. It continues to help people in need.

All four women worked to make changes happen. What they did still makes a difference today.

Index

Barton, Clara, 13–15

"Battle Hymn of the Republic," 8, 9

Civil War, 2, 3, 5, 7, 9, 11, 12, 13

Howe, Julia Ward, 7–9

Howe, Samuel Gridley, 7

Lincoln, Abraham, 3, 6

Red Cross, 13, 14, 15

rights, 2, 4, 9

slavery, 2, 4, 5, 7, 10, 11

Truth, Sojourner, 4–6

Tubman, Harriet, 10–12

Underground Railroad, 10